HAL•LEONARD®

# GUITAR PLAY-ALONG

AUDIO ACCESS INCLUDED

# NIRVANA

Photo: Chris Cuffaro, courtesy of The David Geffen Company

Tracking, mixing, and mastering by
Jake Johnson & Bill Maynard at
Paradyme Productions
All guitars by Doug Boduch
Bass by Tom McGirr
Drums by Scott Schroedl

**PLAYBACK+**
Speed • Pitch • Balance • Loop

To access audio visit:
**www.halleonard.com/mylibrary**

Enter Code
7248-1313-8288-4787

ISBN 978-1-4234-2864-0

HAL•LEONARD®

Visit Hal Leonard Online at
**www.halleonard.com**

Contact Us:
**Hal Leonard**
7777 West Bluemound Road
Milwaukee, WI 53213
Email: info@halleonard.com

In Europe contact:
**Hal Leonard Europe Limited**
42 Wigmore Street
Marylebone, London, W1U 2RN
Email: info@halleonardeurope.com

In Australia contact:
**Hal Leonard Australia Pty. Ltd.**
4 Lentara Court
Cheltenham, Victoria, 3192 Australia
Email: info@halleonard.com.au

HAL•LEONARD®

GUITAR
PLAY-ALONG

AUDIO
ACCESS
INCLUDED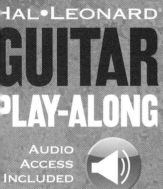

VOL. 78

NIRVANA

## CONTENTS

# Guitar Notation Legend

**THE MUSICAL STAFF** shows pitches and rhythms and is divided by bar lines into measures. Pitches are named after the first seven letters of the alphabet.

**TABLATURE** graphically represents the guitar fingerboard. Each horizontal line represents a string, and each number represents a fret.

4th string, 2nd fret     1st & 2nd strings open, played together     open D chord

**HALF-STEP BEND:** Strike the note and bend up 1/2 step.

**WHOLE-STEP BEND:** Strike the note and bend up one step.

**GRACE NOTE BEND:** Strike the note and bend up as indicated. The first note does not take up any time.

**SLIGHT (MICROTONE) BEND:** Strike the note and bend up 1/4 step.

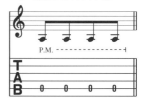

**BEND AND RELEASE:** Strike the note and bend up as indicated, then release back to the original note. Only the first note is struck.

**PRE-BEND:** Bend the note as indicated, then strike it.

**VIBRATO:** The string is vibrated by rapidly bending and releasing the note with the fretting hand.

**PALM MUTING:** The note is partially muted by the pick hand lightly touching the string(s) just before the bridge.

**HAMMER-ON:** Strike the first (lower) note with one finger, then sound the higher note (on the same string) with another finger by fretting it without picking.

**PULL-OFF:** Place both fingers on the notes to be sounded. Strike the first note and without picking, pull the finger off to sound the second (lower) note.

**LEGATO SLIDE:** Strike the first note and then slide the same fret-hand finger up or down to the second note. The second note is not struck.

**SHIFT SLIDE:** Same as legato slide, except the second note is struck.

**TRILL:** Very rapidly alternate between the notes indicated by continuously hammering on and pulling off.

**TAPPING:** Hammer ("tap") the fret indicated with the pick-hand index or middle finger and pull off to the note fretted by the fret hand.

**NATURAL HARMONIC:** Strike the note while the fret-hand lightly touches the string directly over the fret indicated.

**PINCH HARMONIC:** The note is fretted normally and a harmonic is produced by adding the edge of the thumb or the tip of the index finger of the pick hand to the normal pick attack.

**TREMOLO PICKING:** The note is picked as rapidly and continuously as possible.

**VIBRATO BAR DIVE AND RETURN:** The pitch of the note or chord is dropped a specified number of steps (in rhythm) then returned to the original pitch.

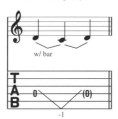

**VIBRATO BAR SCOOP:** Depress the bar just before striking the note, then quickly release the bar.

**VIBRATO BAR DIP:** Strike the note and then immediately drop a specified number of steps, then release back to the original pitch.

# Additional Musical Definitions

 *(accent)* • Accentuate note (play it louder)

 *(staccato)* • Play the note short

***D.S. al Coda*** • Go back to the sign (𝄋), then play until the measure marked "**To Coda**", then skip to the section labelled "**Coda**."

***D.C. al Fine*** • Go back to the beginning of the song and play until the measure marked "***Fine***" (end).

**Fill** • Label used to identify a brief melodic figure which is to be inserted into the arrangement.

**N.C.** • No Chord

 • Repeat measures between signs.

 • When a repeated section has different endings, play the first ending only the first time and the second ending only the second time.

# All Apologies

**Words and Music by Kurt Cobain**

Drop D tuning, down 1/2 step:
(low to high) Db-Ab-Db-Gb-Bb-Eb

**Intro**

**Moderately** ♩ = 112

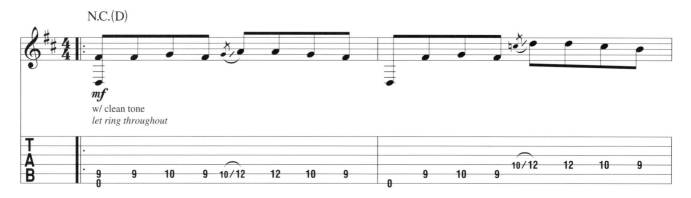

**Verse**

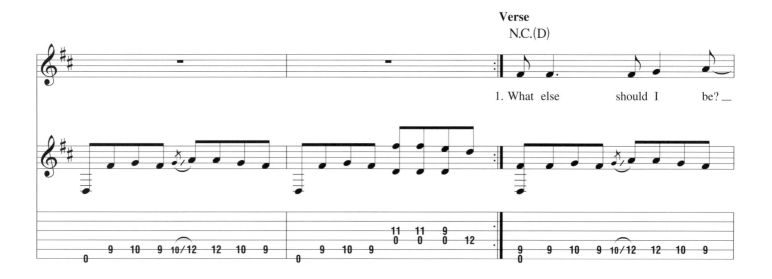

1. What else should I be? __

__ All a - pol - o - gies. __

*w/ random fdbk., next 22 meas.

All a - lone ___ is all ___ we all ___ are. All a - lone ___ is all ___

___ we all ___ are. All a - lone ___ is all ___ we all ___ are.

All a - lone ___ is all ___ we all ___ are. All a - lone ___ is all ___

*dim.*

___ we all ___ are. All a - lone ___ is all ___ we all ___ are.

Gtr. tacet

All a - lone ___ is all ___ we all ___ are. All a - lone ___ is all ___ we all ___ are.

# Come as You Are

**Words and Music by Kurt Cobain**

Tune down one step:
(low to high) D-G-C-F-A-D

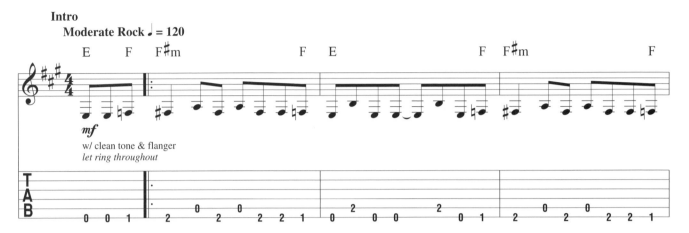

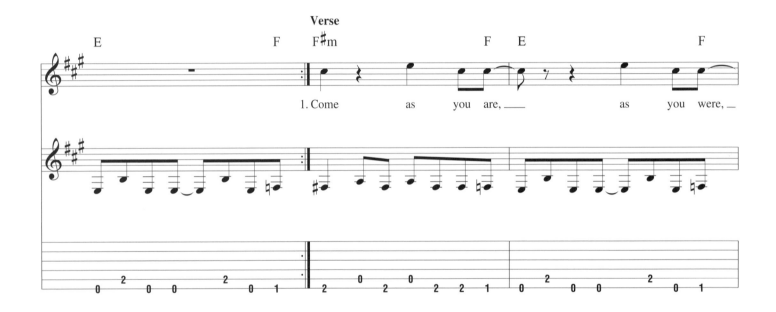

No, I don't _____ have a gun. _____ No, I don't _

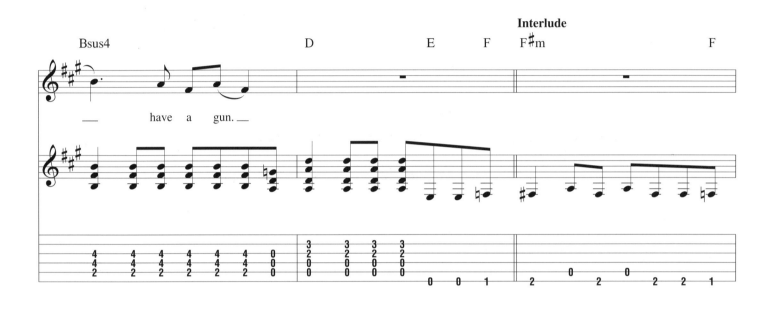

_ have a gun. _____

**Interlude**

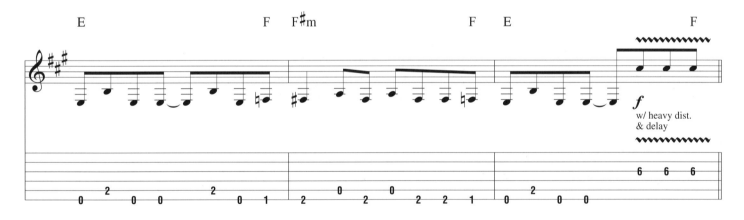

w/ heavy dist.
& delay

**Guitar Solo**

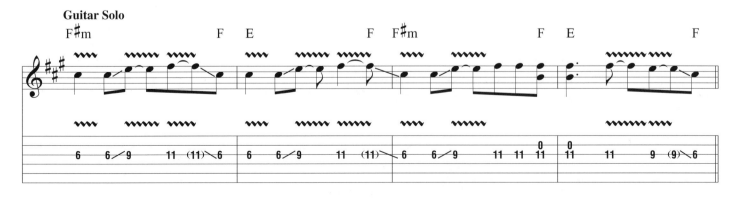

18

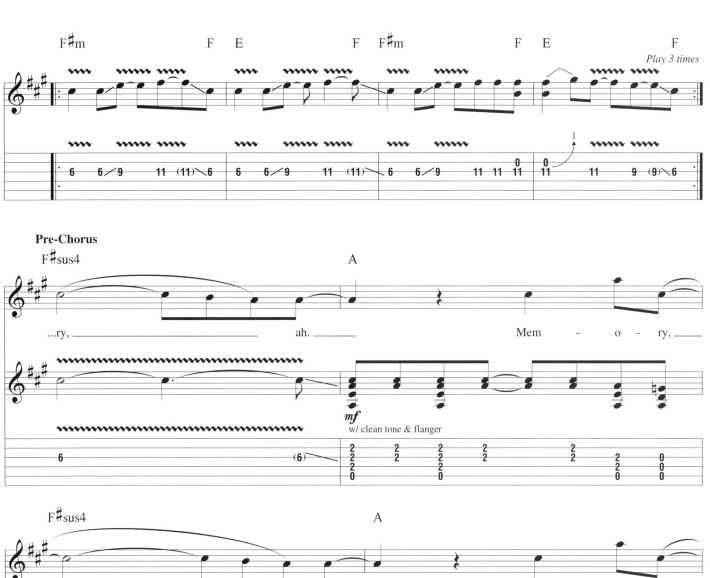

## Pre-Chorus

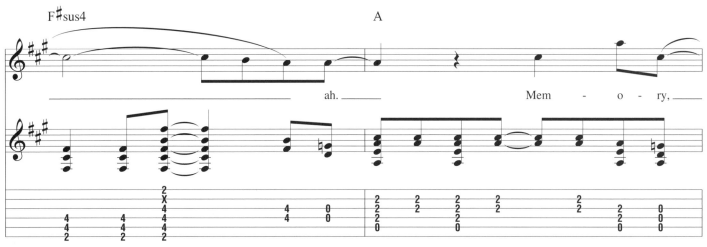

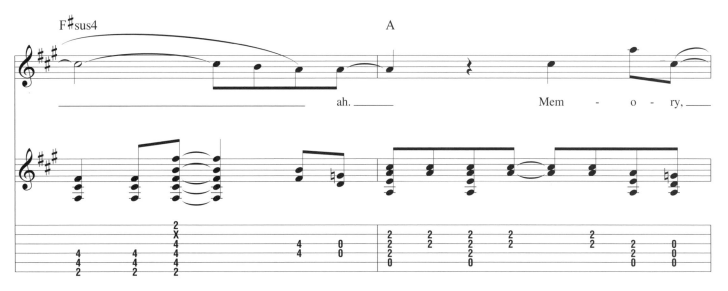

# Dumb

**Words and Music by Kurt Cobain**

Tune down 1/2 step:
(low to high) E♭-A♭-D♭-G♭-B♭-E♭

**Verse**

**Moderately** ♩ = 114

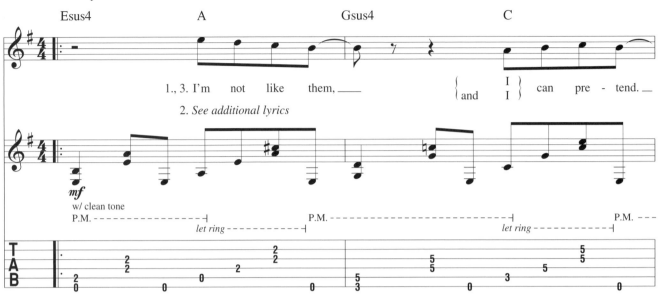

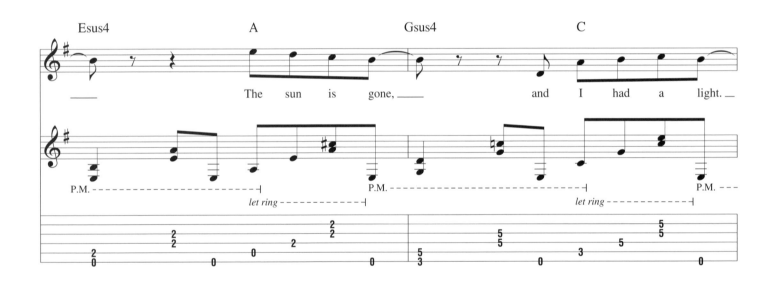

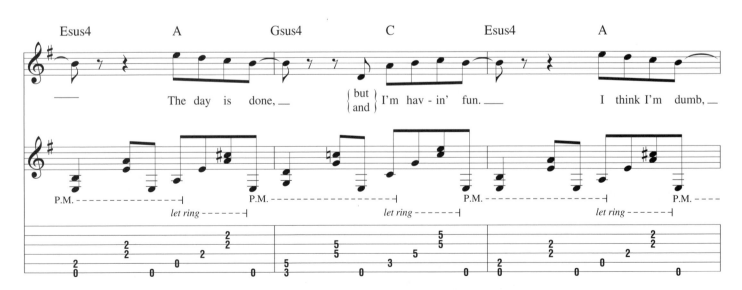

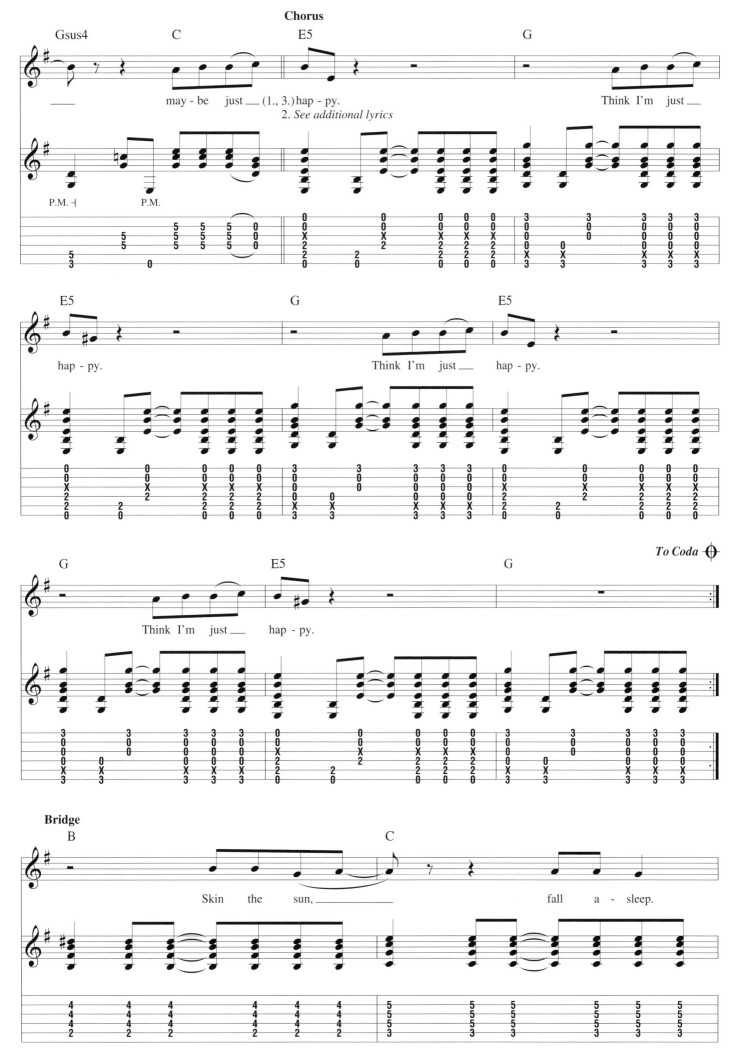

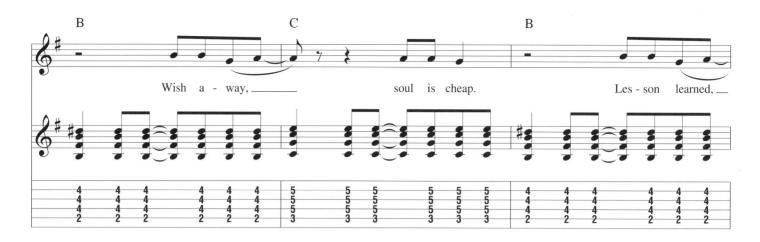

Wish a - way, _____ soul is cheap. Les - son learned, ___

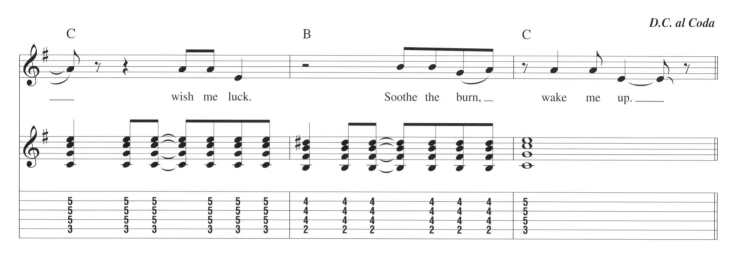

*D.C. al Coda*

____ wish me luck. Soothe the burn, ___ wake me up. ___

**⊕ Coda**
**Outro**

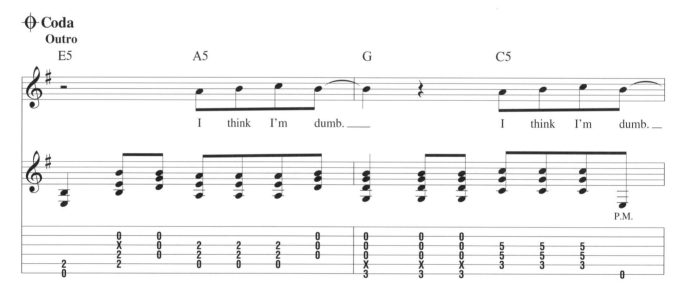

I think I'm dumb. ____ I think I'm dumb. __

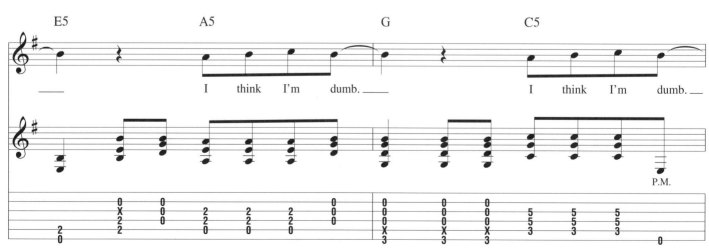

____ I think I'm dumb. ____ I think I'm dumb. __

*Additional Lyrics*

2. My heart is broke, and I have some glue.
   Help me inhale, mend it with you.
   We'll float around, hang out on clouds.
   Then we'll come down,

*Chorus* 2. Have a hangover.
   And have a hangover.
   Have a hangover.
   Have a hangover.

# In Bloom

**Words and Music by Kurt Cobain**

**Intro**

**Moderately slow Rock** ♩ = 78

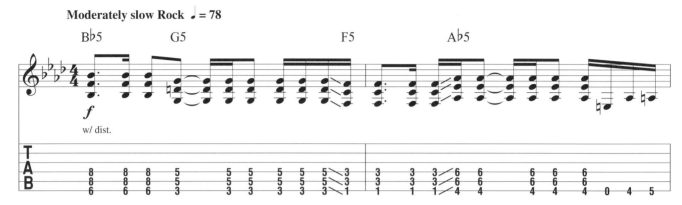

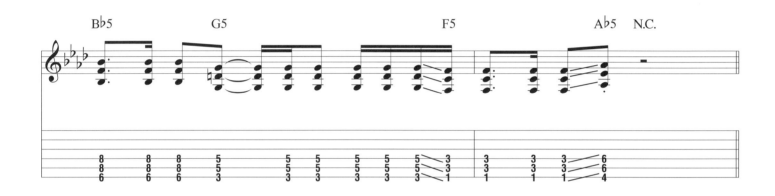

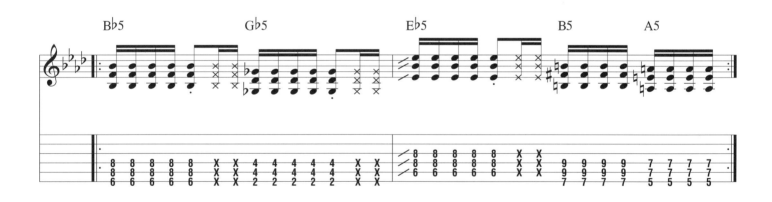

**Verse**

Gtr. tacet

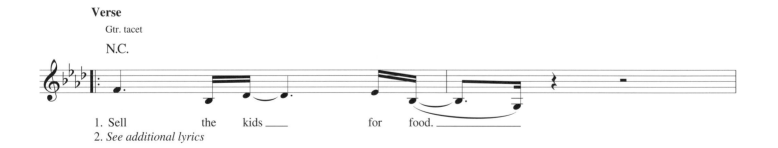

1. Sell the kids _____ for food. _____
2. *See additional lyrics*

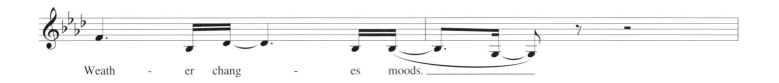

Weath - er chang - es moods. _____

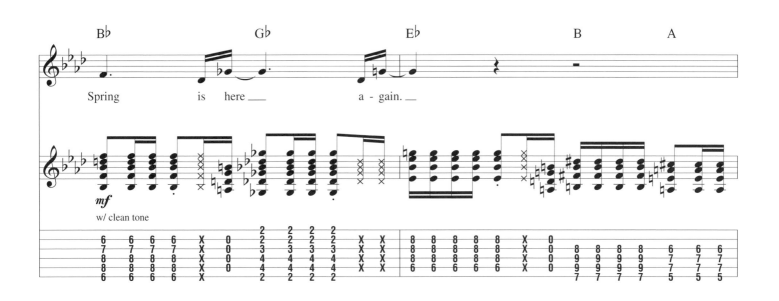

Spring is here ___ a - gain. ___

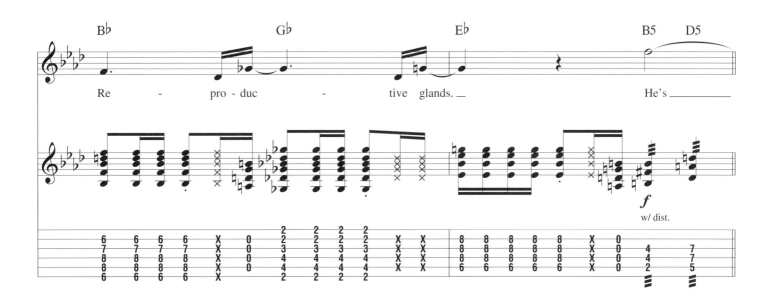

Re - pro - duc - tive glands. __ He's ___

**𝄋 Chorus**

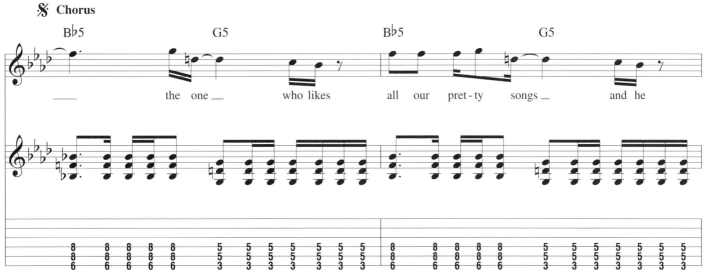

___ the one ___ who likes all our pret - ty songs ___ and he

**Guitar Solo**

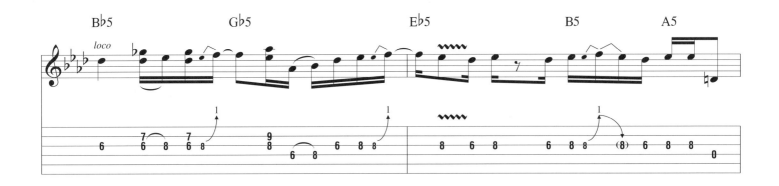

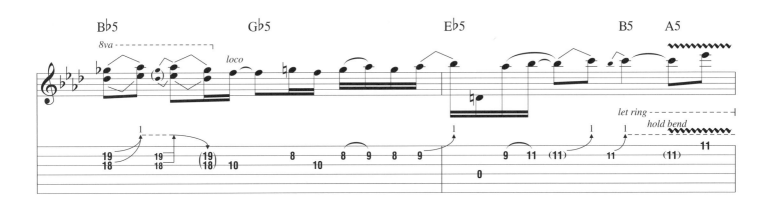

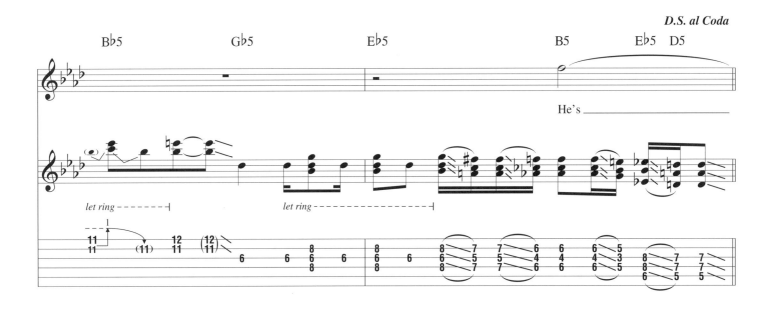

don't    know      what    it      means, __

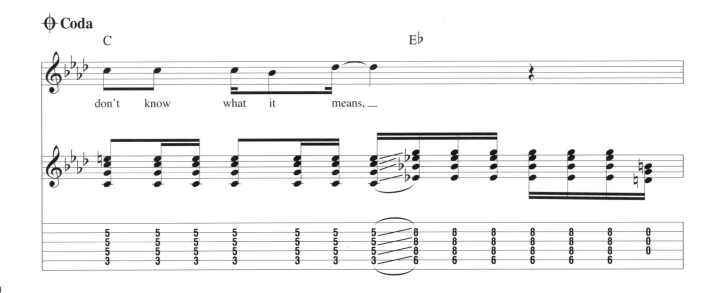

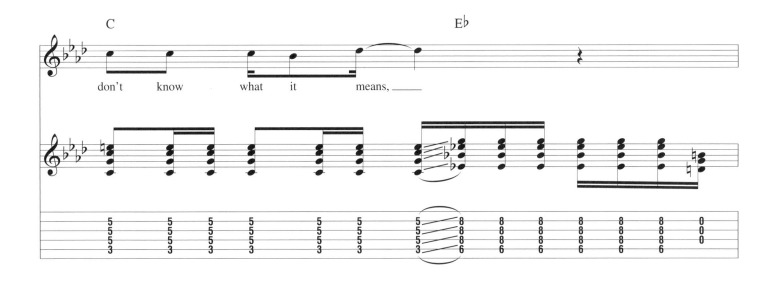

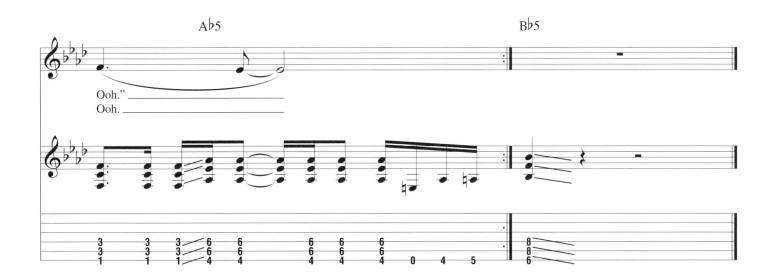

*Additional Lyrics*

2. We can have some more.
Nature is a whore.
Bruises on the fruit.
Tender age in bloom.

# Smells Like Teen Spirit

**Words and Music by Kurt Cobain, Krist Novoselic and Dave Grohl**

Intro
**Driving Rock** ♩ = 116

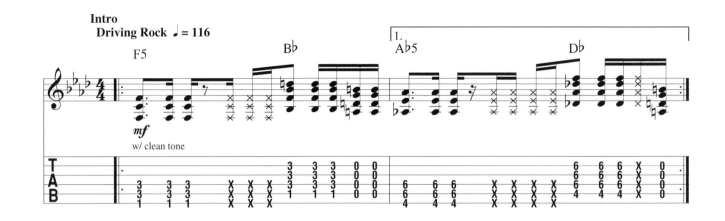

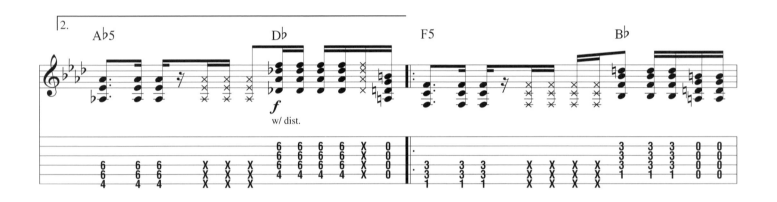

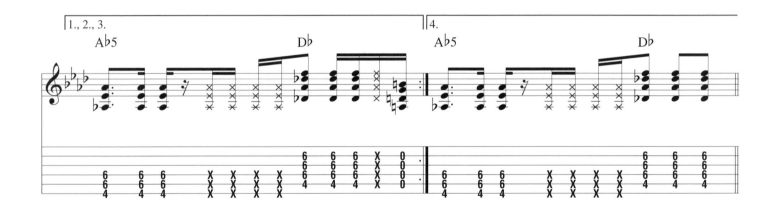

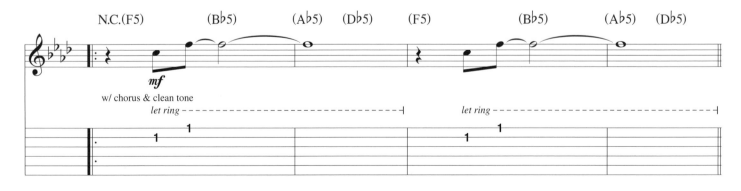

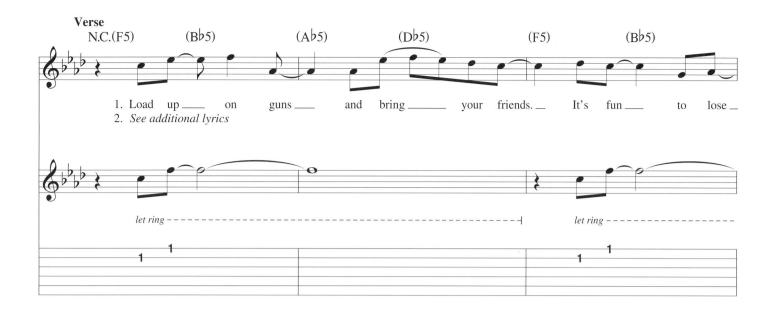

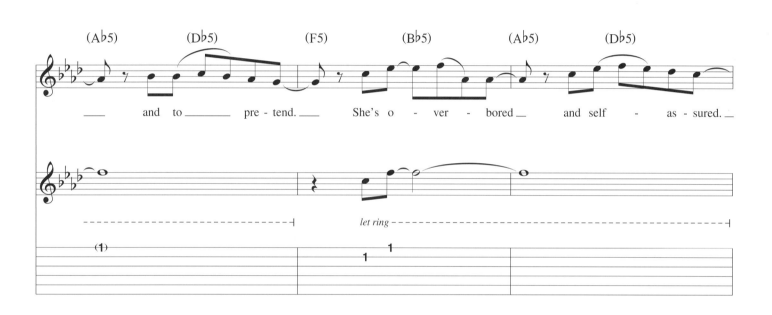

**Pre-Chorus**

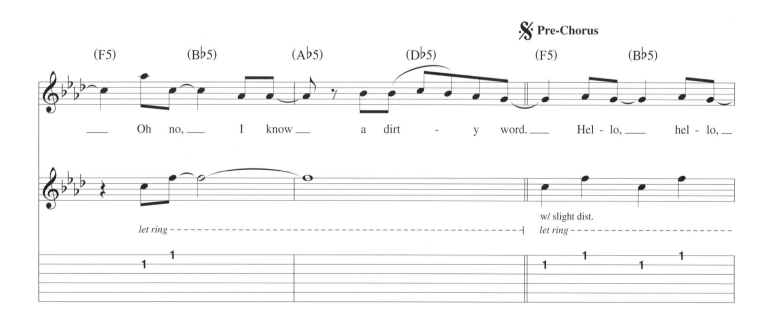

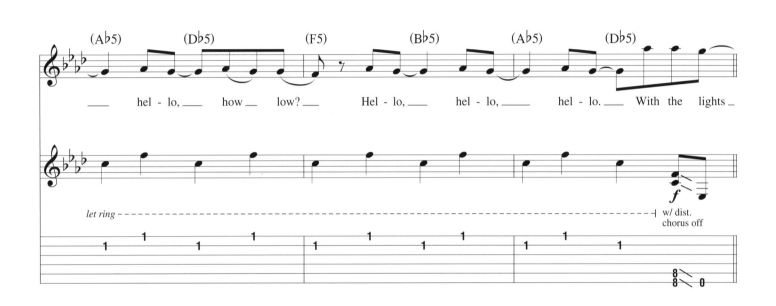

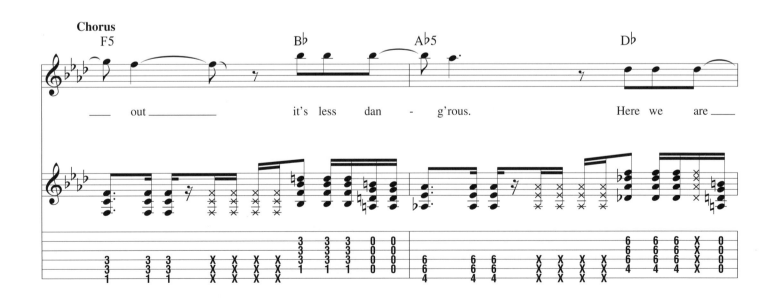

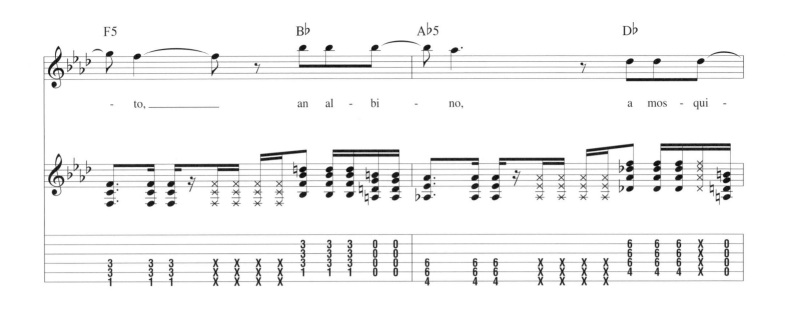

to, _____ an al - bi - no, a mos - qui -

*To Coda* ⊕

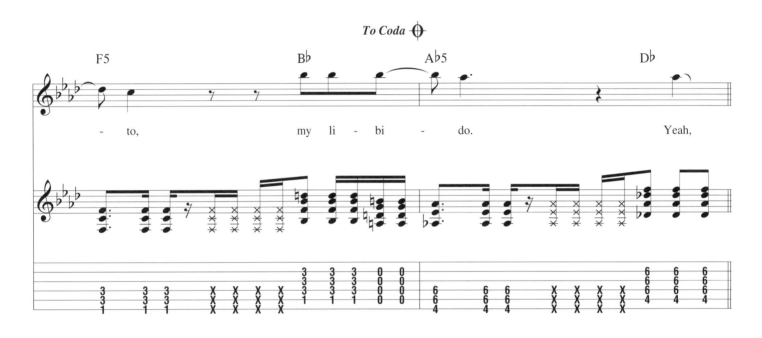

- to, my li - bi - do. Yeah,

**Bridge**

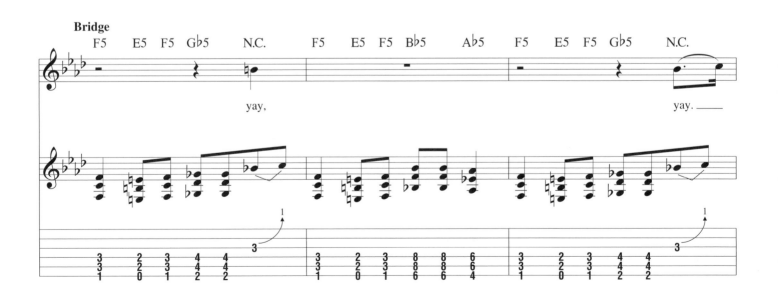

yay, yay. \_\_\_\_\_

*Additional Lyrics*

2. I'm worse at what I do best,
And for this gift I feel blessed.
Our little group has always been
And always will until the end.

# Heart Shaped Box

**Words and Music by Kurt Cobain**

Drop D tuning, down 1/2 step:
(low to high) Db-Ab-Db-Gb-Bb-Eb

**Intro**

**Moderately** ♩ = 100

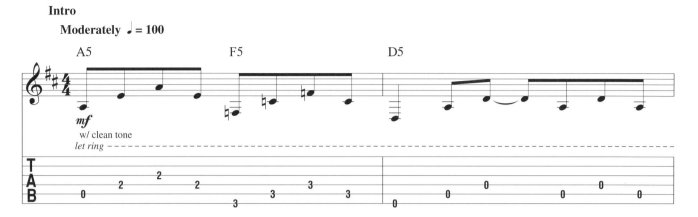

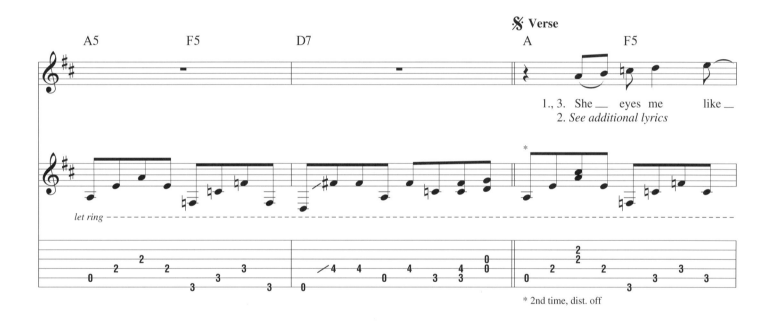

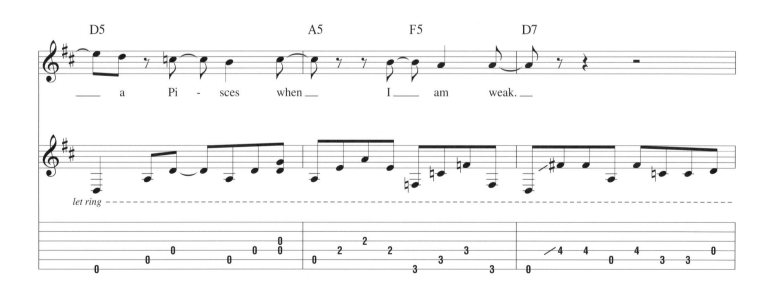

**Chorus**

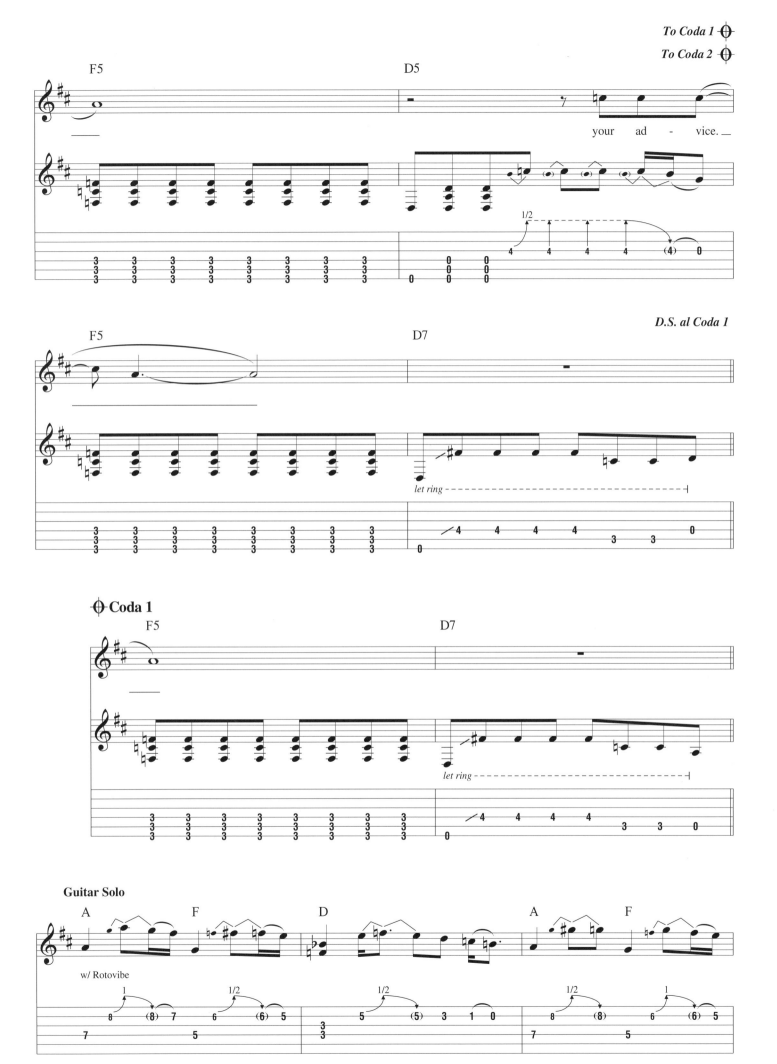

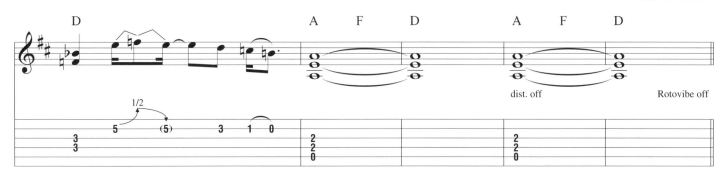

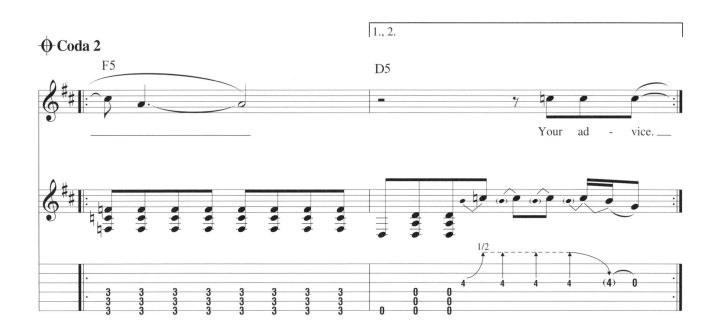

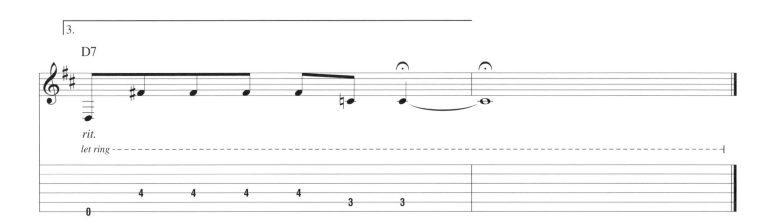

*Additional Lyrics*

2. Meat-eating orchids forgive no one just yet.
   Cut myself on angel's hair and baby's breath.
   Broken hymen of your highness, I'm left black.
   Throw down your umbilical noose so I can climb right back.

# Lithium
### Words and Music by Kurt Cobain

Tune down 1 step:
(low to high) D-G-C-F-A-D

**Intro**

**Moderate Rock** ♩ = 124

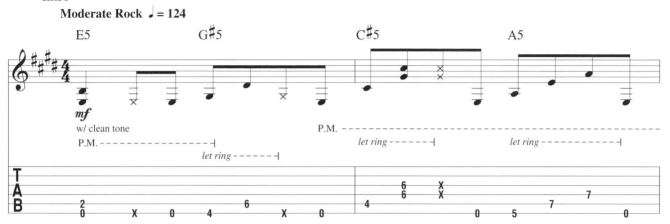

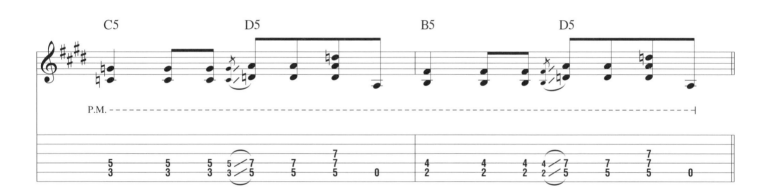

**𝄌 Verse**

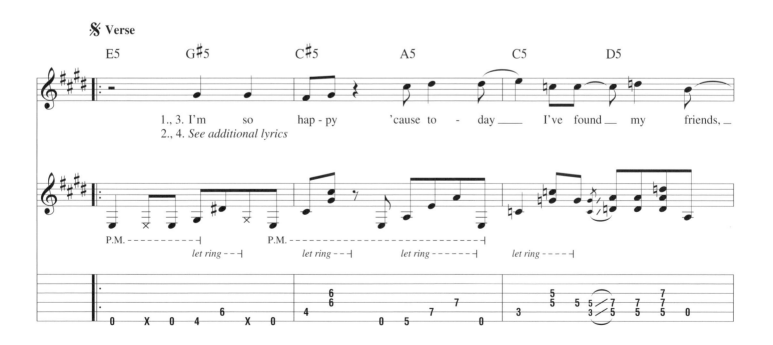

1., 3. I'm so hap-py 'cause to-day ___ I've found ___ my friends, ___
2., 4. *See additional lyrics*

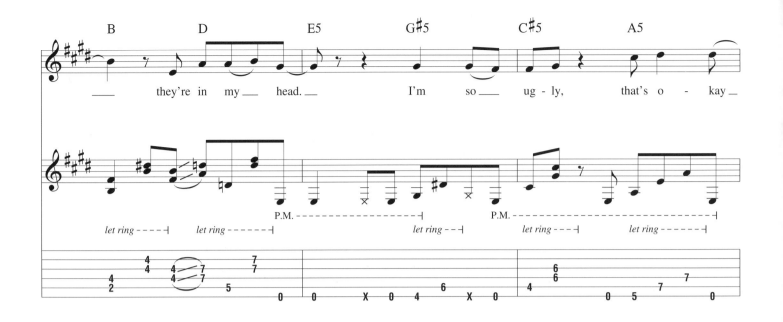

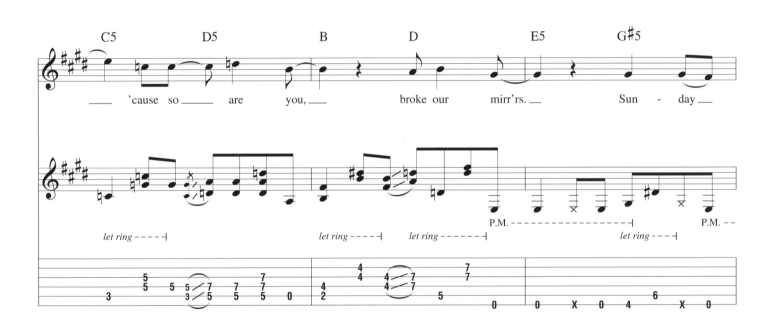

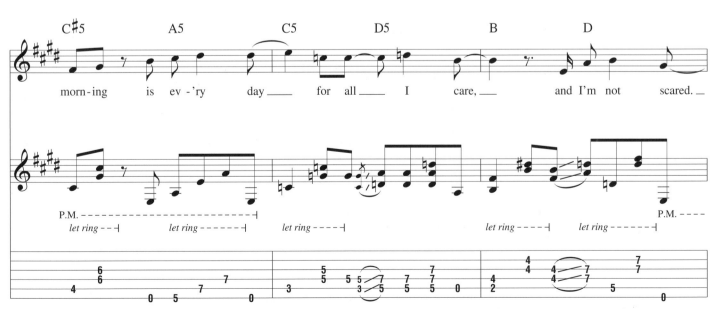

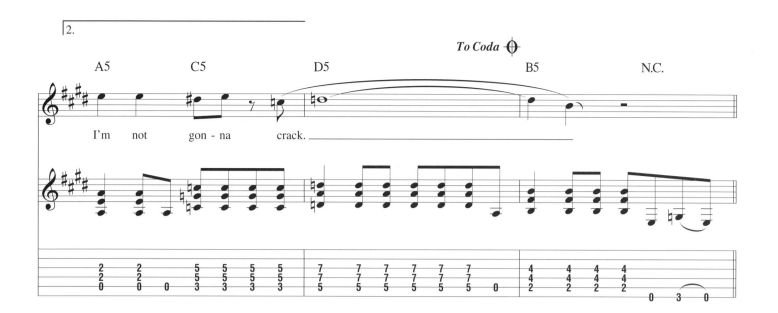

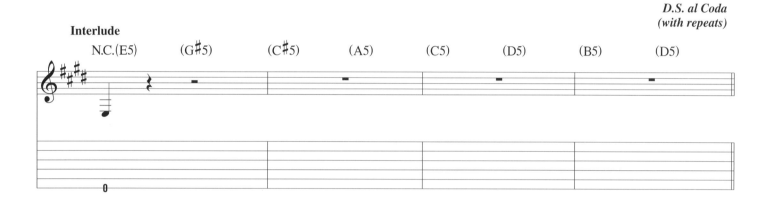

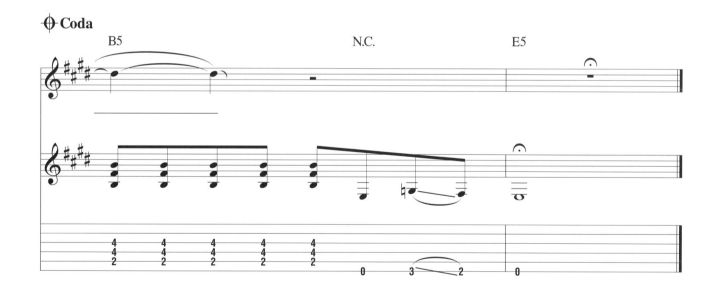

*Additional Lyrics*

2., 4. I'm so lonely; that's okay,
I shaved my head,
And I'm not sad.
And just maybe I'm to blame for all I've heard,
But I'm not sure.
I'm so excited, I can't wait to meet you there,
But I don't care.
I'm so horny; that's okay, my will is good.

# Rape Me

**Words and Music by Kurt Cobain**

Tune down 1/2 step:
(low to high) E♭-A♭-D♭-G♭-B♭-E♭

**Intro**

**Moderately** ♩ = 112

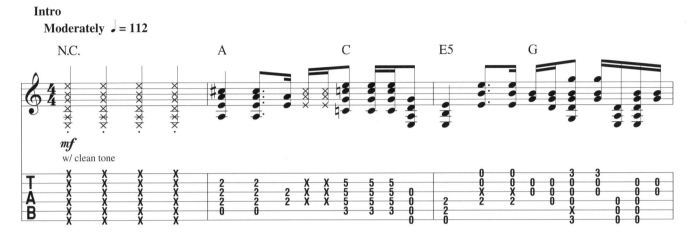

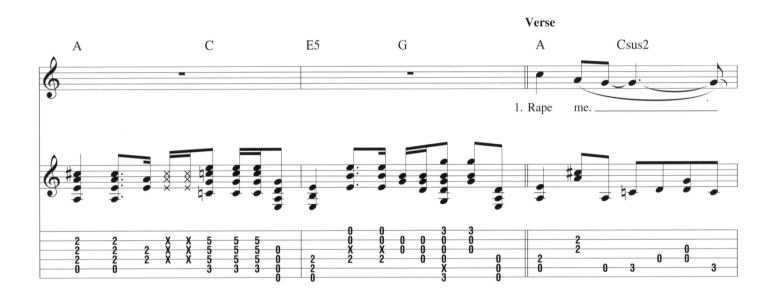

1. Rape me. _____

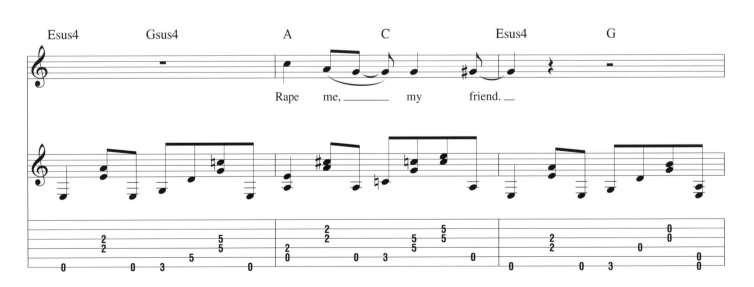

Rape me, _____ my friend. _____

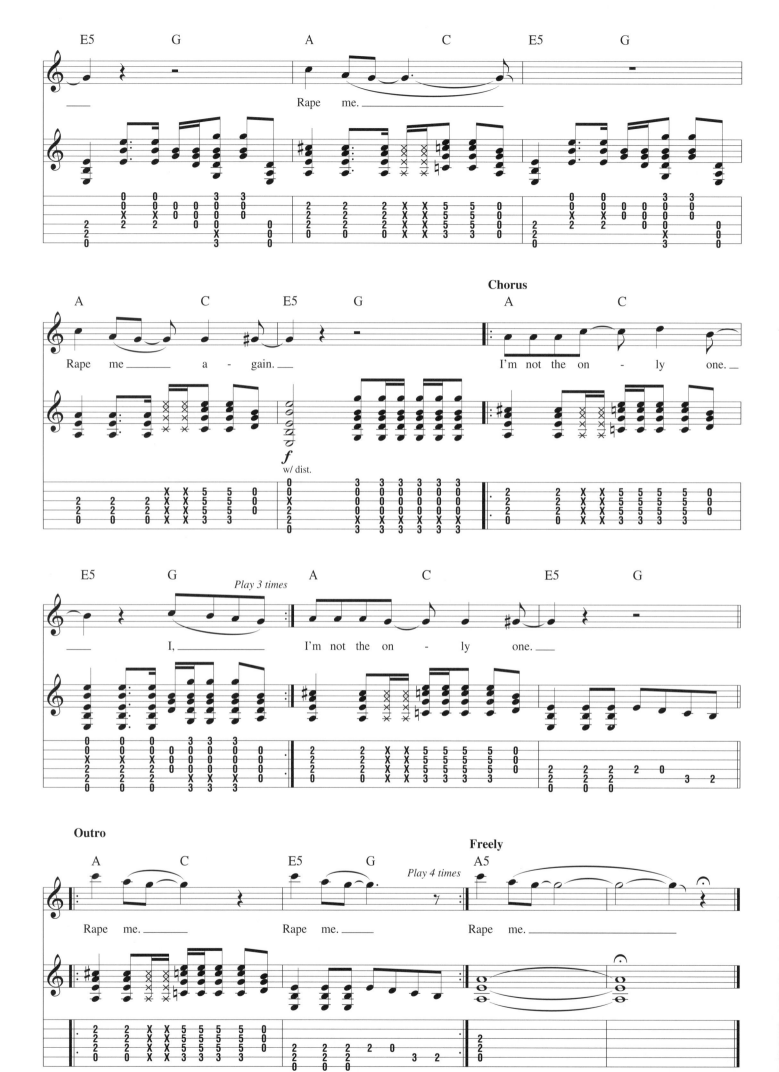

# HAL•LEONARD GUITAR PLAY-ALONG

This series will help you play your favorite songs quickly and easily. Just follow the tab and listen to the audio to the hear how the guitar should sound, and then play along using the separate backing tracks. Audio files also include software to slow down the tempo without changing pitch. The melody and lyrics are included in the book so that you can sing or simply follow along.

**INCLUDES TAB**

Complete song lists available online.

Prices, contents, and availability subject to change without notice.

www.halleonard.com

# RECORDED VERSIONS®

## The Best Note-For-Note Transcriptions Available

**AUTHENTIC TRANSCRIPTIONS WITH NOTES AND TABLATURE**

| | | |
|---|---|---|
| 00690603 | Aerosmith – O Yeah! Ultimate Hits ... | $29.99 |
| 00690178 | Alice in Chains – Acoustic ................. | $22.99 |
| 00694865 | Alice in Chains – Dirt ........................ | $19.99 |
| 00694925 | Alice in Chains – Jar of Flies/Sap...... | $19.99 |
| 00691091 | Alice Cooper – Best of ...................... | $24.99 |
| 00690958 | Duane Allman – Guitar Anthology ..... | $29.99 |
| 00694932 | Allman Brothers Band – Volume 1..... | $29.99 |
| 00694933 | Allman Brothers Band – Volume 2..... | $27.99 |
| 00694934 | Allman Brothers Band – Volume 3..... | $29.99 |
| 00690945 | Alter Bridge – Blackbird ................... | $24.99 |
| 00123558 | Arctic Monkeys – AM ........................ | $24.99 |
| 00214869 | Avenged Sevenfold – Best of 2005-2013 ....................... | $29.99 |
| 00690489 | Beatles – 1 ...................................... | $24.99 |
| 00694929 | Beatles – 1962-1966 ........................ | $27.99 |
| 00694930 | Beatles – 1967-1970 ........................ | $29.99 |
| 00694880 | Beatles – Abbey Road ...................... | $19.99 |
| 00694832 | Beatles – Acoustic Guitar.................. | $27.99 |
| 00690110 | Beatles – White Album (Book 1)........ | $19.99 |
| 00692385 | Chuck Berry ..................................... | $24.99 |
| 00147787 | Black Crowes – Best of ..................... | $24.99 |
| 00690149 | Black Sabbath .................................. | $19.99 |
| 00690901 | Black Sabbath – Best of ................... | $22.99 |
| 00691010 | Black Sabbath – Heaven and Hell .... | $24.99 |
| 00690148 | Black Sabbath – Master of Reality .... | $19.99 |
| 00690142 | Black Sabbath – Paranoid ................. | $19.99 |
| 00148544 | Michael Bloomfield – Guitar Anthology ............................. | $24.99 |
| 00158600 | Joe Bonamassa – Blues of Desperation | $24.99 |
| 00198117 | Joe Bonamassa – Muddy Wolf at Red Rocks............... | $24.99 |
| 00283540 | Joe Bonamassa – Redemption ......... | $24.99 |
| 00358863 | Joe Bonamassa – Royal Tea ............. | $24.99 |
| 00690913 | Boston ............................................. | $22.99 |
| 00690491 | David Bowie – Best of ....................... | $22.99 |
| 00286503 | Big Bill Broonzy – Guitar Collection .. | $19.99 |
| 00690261 | The Carter Family Collection ............ | $19.99 |
| 00691079 | Johnny Cash – Best of ...................... | $24.99 |
| 00690936 | Eric Clapton – Complete Clapton ...... | $34.99 |
| 00694869 | Eric Clapton – Unplugged ................. | $24.99 |
| 00124873 | Eric Clapton – Unplugged (Deluxe) ... | $29.99 |
| 00138731 | Eric Clapton & Friends – The Breeze | $24.99 |
| 00139967 | Coheed & Cambria – In Keeping Secrets of Silent Earth: 3 .................. | $24.99 |
| 00141704 | Jesse Cook – Works, Vol. 1 ............. | $19.99 |
| 00288787 | Creed – Greatest Hits....................... | $22.99 |
| 00690819 | Creedence Clearwater Revival .......... | $27.99 |
| 00690648 | Jim Croce – Very Best of................... | $19.99 |
| 00690572 | Steve Cropper – Soul Man ................ | $22.99 |
| 00690613 | Crosby, Stills & Nash – Best of........ | $29.99 |
| 00690784 | Def Leppard – Best of ...................... | $24.99 |
| 00694831 | Derek and the Dominos – Layla & Other Assorted Love Songs .. | $24.99 |
| 00291164 | Dream Theater – Distance Over Time | $24.99 |
| 00278631 | Eagles – Greatest Hits 1971-1975 ..... | $22.99 |
| 00278632 | Eagles – Very Best of........................ | $39.99 |
| 00690515 | Extreme II – Pornograffiti.................. | $24.99 |
| 00150257 | John Fahey – Guitar Anthology ......... | $24.99 |
| 00690664 | Fleetwood Mac – Best of.................... | $24.99 |
| 00691024 | Foo Fighters – Greatest Hits ............. | $24.99 |
| 00120220 | Robben Ford – Guitar Anthology ....... | $29.99 |
| 00295410 | Rory Gallagher – Blues .................... | $24.99 |
| 00139460 | Grateful Dead – Guitar Anthology...... | $34.99 |
| 00691190 | Peter Green – Best of ....................... | $24.99 |

| | | |
|---|---|---|
| 00287517 | Greta Van Fleet – Anthem of the Peaceful Army .......... | $22.99 |
| 00287515 | Greta Van Fleet – From the Fires ...... | $19.99 |
| 00694798 | George Harrison – Anthology............ | $24.99 |
| 00692930 | Jimi Hendrix – Are You Experienced? | $29.99 |
| 00692931 | Jimi Hendrix – Axis: Bold As Love .... | $24.99 |
| 00690304 | Jimi Hendrix – Band of Gypsys......... | $27.99 |
| 00694944 | Jimi Hendrix – Blues ........................ | $29.99 |
| 00692932 | Jimi Hendrix – Electric Ladyland...... | $27.99 |
| 00660029 | Buddy Holly – Best of....................... | $24.99 |
| 00200446 | Iron Maiden – Guitar Tab ................. | $34.99 |
| 00694912 | Eric Johnson – Ah Via Musicom ....... | $24.99 |
| 00690271 | Robert Johnson – Transcriptions ...... | $27.99 |
| 00690427 | Judas Priest – Best of ...................... | $24.99 |
| 00690492 | B.B. King – Anthology....................... | $29.99 |
| 00130447 | B.B. King – Live at the Regal ............ | $19.99 |
| 00690134 | Freddie King – Collection ................. | $22.99 |
| 00327968 | Marcus King – El Dorado .................. | $22.99 |
| 00690157 | Kiss – Alive ..................................... | $19.99 |
| 00690356 | Kiss – Alive II .................................. | $24.99 |
| 00291163 | Kiss – Very Best of .......................... | $24.99 |
| 00345767 | Greg Koch – Best of.......................... | $29.99 |
| 00690377 | Kris Kristofferson – Guitar Collection | $22.99 |
| 00690834 | Lamb of God – Ashes of the Wake .... | $24.99 |
| 00690525 | George Lynch – Best of ..................... | $29.99 |
| 00690955 | Lynyrd Skynyrd – All-Time Greatest Hits ..................... | $24.99 |
| 00694954 | Lynyrd Skynyrd – New Best of .......... | $24.99 |
| 00690577 | Yngwie Malmsteen – Anthology ........ | $29.99 |
| 00694896 | John Mayall with Eric Clapton – Blues Breakers ................................ | $19.99 |
| 00694952 | Megadeth – Countdown to Extinction | $24.99 |
| 00276065 | Megadeth – Greatest Hits: Back to the Start ........ | $27.99 |
| 00694951 | Megadeth – Rust in Peace ................ | $27.99 |
| 00690011 | Megadeth – Youthanasia .................. | $24.99 |
| 00209876 | Metallica – Hardwired to Self-Destruct | $24.99 |
| 00690646 | Pat Metheny – One Quiet Night ........ | $24.99 |
| 00102591 | Wes Montgomery – Guitar Anthology | $27.99 |
| 00691092 | Gary Moore – Best of ........................ | $27.99 |
| 00694802 | Gary Moore – Still Got the Blues ...... | $24.99 |
| 00355456 | Alanis Morisette – Jagged Little Pill | $22.99 |
| 00690611 | Nirvana ........................................... | $24.99 |
| 00694913 | Nirvana – In Utero ........................... | $22.99 |
| 00694883 | Nirvana – Nevermind ....................... | $19.99 |
| 00690026 | Nirvana – Unplugged in New York..... | $19.99 |
| 00265439 | Nothing More – Tab Collection .......... | $24.99 |
| 00243349 | Opeth – Best of................................ | $22.99 |
| 00690499 | Tom Petty – Definitive Guitar Collection .............. | $24.99 |
| 00121933 | Pink Floyd – Acoustic Guitar Collection ................ | $27.99 |
| 00690428 | Pink Floyd – Dark Side of the Moon . | $22.99 |
| 00244637 | Pink Floyd – Guitar Anthology .......... | $24.99 |
| 00239799 | Pink Floyd – The Wall ...................... | $27.99 |
| 00690789 | Poison – Best of ............................... | $22.99 |
| 00690925 | Prince – Very Best of........................ | $24.99 |
| 00690003 | Queen – Classic Queen .................... | $24.99 |
| 00694975 | Queen – Greatest Hits ...................... | $25.99 |
| 00694910 | Rage Against the Machine................. | $24.99 |
| 00119834 | Rage Against the Machine – Guitar Anthology .......................... | $24.99 |
| 00690426 | Ratt – Best of................................... | $24.99 |
| 00690055 | Red Hot Chili Peppers – Blood Sugar Sex Magik ................. | $19.99 |

| | | |
|---|---|---|
| 00690379 | Red Hot Chili Peppers – Californication............................... | $22.99 |
| 00690673 | Red Hot Chili Peppers – Greatest Hits | $24.99 |
| 00690852 | Red Hot Chili Peppers – Stadium Arcadium ......................... | $29.99 |
| 00690511 | Django Reinhardt – Definitive Collection .......................... | $24.99 |
| 00690014 | Rolling Stones – Exile on Main Street | $24.99 |
| 00690631 | Rolling Stones – Guitar Anthology .... | $34.99 |
| 00323854 | Rush – The Spirit of Radio: Greatest Hits, 1974-1987................... | $22.99 |
| 00173534 | Santana – Guitar Anthology.............. | $29.99 |
| 00276350 | Joe Satriani – What Happens Next ... | $24.99 |
| 00690566 | Scorpions – Best of .......................... | $24.99 |
| 00690604 | Bob Seger – Guitar Collection .......... | $24.99 |
| 00234543 | Ed Sheeran – Divide* ....................... | $19.99 |
| 00691114 | Slash – Guitar Anthology ................. | $34.99 |
| 00690813 | Slayer – Guitar Collection ................ | $24.99 |
| 00690419 | Slipknot ........................................... | $22.99 |
| 00316982 | Smashing Pumpkins – Greatest Hits . | $24.99 |
| 00690912 | Soundgarden – Guitar Anthology....... | $24.99 |
| 00120004 | Steely Dan – Best of......................... | $27.99 |
| 00322564 | Stone Temple Pilots – Thank You...... | $22.99 |
| 00690520 | Styx – Guitar Collection .................... | $22.99 |
| 00120081 | Sublime ........................................... | $22.99 |
| 00690531 | System of a Down – Toxicity ............. | $19.99 |
| 00694824 | James Taylor – Best of ..................... | $19.99 |
| 00694887 | Thin Lizzy – Best of .......................... | $22.99 |
| 00253237 | Trivium – Guitar Tab Anthology......... | $24.99 |
| 00690683 | Robin Trower – Bridge of Sighs........ | $19.99 |
| 00156024 | Steve Vai – Guitar Anthology ............ | $39.99 |
| 00660137 | Steve Vai – Passion & Warfare ........ | $29.99 |
| 00295076 | Van Halen – 30 Classics ................... | $29.99 |
| 00690024 | Stevie Ray Vaughan – Couldn't Stand the Weather.............. | $22.99 |
| 00660058 | Stevie Ray Vaughan – Lightnin' Blues 1983-1987................. | $29.99 |
| 00217455 | Stevie Ray Vaughan – Plays Slow Blues.............................. | $24.99 |
| 00694835 | Stevie Ray Vaughan – The Sky Is Crying ............................ | $24.99 |
| 00690015 | Stevie Ray Vaughan – Texas Flood ... | $22.99 |
| 00694789 | Muddy Waters – Deep Blues.............. | $27.99 |
| 00152161 | Doc Watson – Guitar Anthology......... | $24.99 |
| 00690071 | Weezer (The Blue Album).................. | $22.99 |
| 00237811 | White Stripes – Greatest Hits ........... | $24.99 |
| 00117511 | Whitesnake – Guitar Collection......... | $24.99 |
| 00122303 | Yes – Guitar Collection ..................... | $24.99 |
| 00690443 | Frank Zappa – Hot Rats .................... | $22.99 |
| 00121684 | ZZ Top – Early Classics .................... | $27.99 |
| 00690589 | ZZ Top – Guitar Anthology ................ | $24.99 |

**COMPLETE SERIES LIST ONLINE!**

# HAL•LEONARD®

www.halleonard.com

Prices and availability subject to change without notice.
*Tab transcriptions only.

0622